Mecca

and Other Islamic Holy Places

Mandy Ross

For information, address the publisher:
Raintree, 100 N. LaSalle, Suite 1200, Chicago, IL 60602

Design by Joanna Sapwell and StoryBooks
Printed and bound in China.

07 06 05 04 03
10 9 8 7 6 5 4 3 2 1

Library of Congress Cataloging-in-Publication Data

Ross, Mandy.
   Mecca / Mandy Ross.
      p. cm. -- (Holy places)
   Summary: An introduction to Islam which focuses on the holy
sites of the religion.
   Includes bibliographical references and index.
   ISBN 0-7398-6080-1 (HC), 1-4109-0053-3 (Pbk.)
   1. Mecca (Saudi Arabia)--Juvenile literature. 2. Islam--Juvenile
literature.   [1. Mecca (Saudi Arabia) 2. Islam.]   I. Title.
II. Series.
   DS248.M4R67 2003
   953.8--dc21

2002014531

Acknowledgments
The Publishers would like to thank the following for permission to reproduce photographs: Associated Press pp. 15, 27; Christine Osborne Pictures p. 9; Corbis p. 29; Popperfoto pp. 10, 14, 18, 19, 21; Robert Harding Picture Library p. 26; Trip/A Farago p. 28; Trip/H Rogers pp. 12, 23, 24, 25; Trip/Trip pp. 5, 6, 7, 8, 11, 13, 16, 17, 20.

Cover photograph reproduced with permission of The Stock Market.

Every effort has been made to contact copyright holders of any material reproduced in this book. Any omissions will be rectified in subsequent printings if notice is given to the Publisher.

Contents

Words printed in bold letters, **like this**, are explained in the Glossary on page 30.

What Is Mecca?

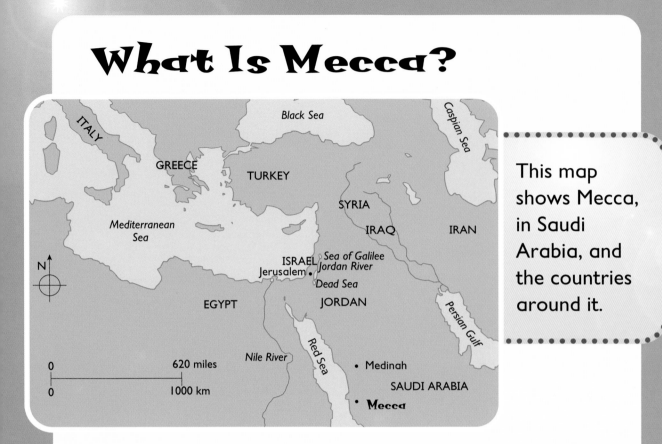

ITALY

Black Sea

Caspian Sea

GREECE

TURKEY

SYRIA

Mediterranean
Sea

IRAQ

IRAN

ISRAEL
Jerusalem

Sea of Galilee
Jordan River

Dead Sea

EGYPT

JORDAN

Persian Gulf

N

Nile River

Red Sea

Medinah

SAUDI ARABIA

Mecca

0   620 miles
0   1000 km

This map shows Mecca, in Saudi Arabia, and the countries around it.

Mecca is the **holiest** city for Muslims, people who follow the **religion** of **Islam.** Mecca is in the country we now call Saudi Arabia, in the **Middle East.** All around the world, Muslims **pray** facing in the direction of Mecca.

Mecca is important to Muslims because their **prophet** Muhammad (**pbuh**) was born there in 570 C.E.

Every year, more than 2 million people make a holy journey or **pilgrimage** to Mecca. They say special prayers as they visit the holy places there. This pilgrimage is called **Hajj.** Every Muslim hopes to go on Hajj to Mecca at least once in his or her life.

What is Islam?

Islam is the religion followed by people called Muslims. Muslims pray to one God, **Allah.** They believe that Allah sent Muhammad (pbuh) to teach people how to live. The Muslim holy book is called the **Qur'an.**

The letters "pbuh" stand for "peace be upon him." Muslims always say these words after Muhammad's name to show their respect for him.

A Muslim place of worship is called a **mosque** (or sometimes masjid). Muslims always pray facing Mecca, so each mosque is built to face this holy city.

Today, Mecca is a modern city. It lies in a desert and is very hot and dry–it hardly ever rains there.

This is the city of Mecca today.

Mecca in Ancient Times

Desert mountains surround Mecca.

Mecca has been an important **holy** place for thousands of years. Muslims believe that the **prophet** Aadam built the first house of **Allah** there, thousands of years before Muhammad (**pbuh**) was born.

Many years later, the prophet Ibrahim lived in the area with his wife, Hajra. The **Qur'an,** tells how Hajra was stranded alone in the hot desert with her baby son, Isma'il. Soon, the baby needed water. Hajra ran between the hills, searching for water. Suddenly, Hajra saw water bubbling

out of the ground. A **miracle** had saved her baby. The spring became known as the Well of Zamzam. Later, Ibrahim built a holy building there. That building was called the Ka'bah.

Mecca grew up around the Well and the Ka'bah. Desert people visited the Ka'bah as a holy place. Great fairs were held nearby each year, and traders sold expensive spices and jewels.

Street stalls sell food to **pilgrims** on **Hajj,** as in ancient times.

The Bible and the Qur'an

Muslims believe that Muhammad (pbuh) was the last in a long line of prophets sent to Earth by Allah. Many of the same prophets appear in the **Jewish** holy book called the **Hebrew Bible.** This is holy to **Christians,** too, who call it the Old Testament.

Names in Bible	Names in Qur'an
Adam	Aadam
Abraham	Ibrahim
Hagar	Hajra
Ishmael	Isma'il
Gabriel	Jibril

Who Was the Prophet Muhammad (pbuh)?

In about 570 C.E., the **prophet** Muhammad (**pbuh**) was born in Mecca. Muhammad (pbuh) was born into a wealthy family. He grew up to be kind and honest. People called him Al-Amin, which means "the trustworthy one."

Muhammad (pbuh) hated to see people worshiping many different gods, cheating the poor, and fighting with one another. He started to go out into the desert beyond Mecca to think and **pray.**

One night in the desert, Muhammad (pbuh) was visited by the Angel Jibril. Jibril carried a piece of cloth with writing on it. Muhammad (pbuh) found that he could read the words, although he had never learned to read or write.

Pilgrims visit the cave where Muhammad (pbuh) stayed in the desert.

People from the desert travel with camels as they did in the time of Muhammad (pbuh).

These words were the first part of the Muslim **holy** book, the **Qur'an.** The angel returned several times to tell Muhammad (pbuh) the rest of the Qur'an.

After that, Muhammad (pbuh) spent his time teaching people about **Allah.** But many people in Mecca did not want to listen. In 622 C.E., Muhammad (pbuh) traveled from Mecca to live and teach in another city called Medinah. Those that followed him there became the first Muslims.

The hijrah and the Muslim calendar

The hijrah is the name for the journey Muhammad (pbuh) made from Mecca to Medinah in 622 C.E. It was so important that the Muslim calendar starts from this year. Muslim years are followed by AH, which comes from words that mean "year of the hijrah."

What Is Mecca's History?

From the age of 40, Muhammad (**pbuh**) spent his life teaching about **Allah** and **Islam**. He died in 632 C.E. After his death, Islam spread quickly to the lands around the Mediterranean Sea. Mecca became the most important place for Muslims everywhere.

Pilgrims came there on **pilgrimage**, or **Hajj,** from all over the world. The pilgrims spent money and Mecca grew rich, as local people sold goods to the people on Hajj.

The Great **Mosque** in Mecca is surrounded by modern buildings.

There have been many battles for control of the land around Mecca. In the centuries after the death of Muhammad (pbuh), Arab rulers, called the Abbasids, were in control. Later, Turkish rulers, called the Ottomans, took over. They were in control for hundreds of years.

In 1932, the kingdom in which Mecca lies was renamed Saudi Arabia. Saudi Arabia is a rich country because it produces and sells oil.

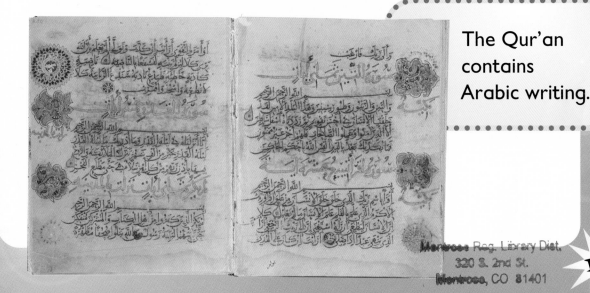

The Qur'an contains Arabic writing.

11

What Is the Great Mosque at Mecca?

The Great **Mosque** is the most important **religious** building in Mecca. Around 500,000 people can fit inside it. The Great Mosque has towers, called minarets, at each corner. From the minarets, the **muezzin,** or caller, calls people to **prayer.**

The Mosque is surrounded by a great wall. The area inside the wall is called the Haram or **holy** enclosure. Inside the Haram is a huge open courtyard paved with white marble. At its center is the Ka'bah, an ancient building in the shape of a huge cube.

Pilgrims pray around the Ka'bah.

The Ka'bah is covered with decorated cloth. The towers behind it are minarets.

The Ka'bah is 49 feet (15 meters) high. It is built of stone, and has a brass door on one side decorated with religious writings from the **Qur'an.** There is a holy black stone in one corner of the Ka'bah. The Ka'bah is covered with a beautiful cloth embroidered with religious writings. Next to the Ka'bah is Hajra's grave and the graves of other **prophets.**

The Great Mosque is a modern building. It has been rebuilt many times over the centuries, each time to make a new and beautiful building to worship **Allah** in. Rebuilding has made it safer for the millions of **pilgrims** who come to Mecca on **Hajj.**

What Is Hajj?

Hajj is the journey to Mecca and is one of the most important things that Muslims believe in. It is one of the "Five Pillars of Islam," which are explained later on page 22.

Before they set off, Muslims get ready to go on Hajj. They say special **prayers** and study the rules for living on Hajj.

Pilgrims travel to Mecca from countries all over the world. Some people save up money over many years to make the journey. In the past, many pilgrims from faraway countries traveled over land and sea for months, or even years, to reach Mecca.

Pilgrims sit with their luggage at Jeddah airport on the journey to Mecca.

These pilgrims are making their way to Mecca on foot.

Today, most pilgrims travel to Saudi Arabia by airplane. After they arrive at Jeddah airport, there is a car trip of about 47 miles (75 kilometers) to Mecca. City officials make special travel arrangements so that all the people can arrive safely on Hajj. Special bus stops and information centers are set up. Police patrol to help travelers and to make sure there is no trouble. There is even a special mail system set up for the period of Hajj.

A long journey

Air travel has made going on Hajj easier than before. Even so, it can still be a long and tiring journey to reach Mecca. But pilgrims see this journey as a **symbol** of their journey toward **Allah.** They do not expect it to be an easy journey.

On Hajj at Mecca

Over two million people arrive at Mecca on **Hajj** each year. They come during the Muslim month of Dhul-Hijja. All of the **pilgrims** wear simple white robes called ihram. Dressing simply shows that everyone, rich or poor, is equal before **Allah.**

A whole city of tents is set up for people to stay in. While they are on Hajj, pilgrims must live very simply. They should not kill any animals, insects, or plants, and they must not do anything unkind or dishonest to anyone. Husbands and wives must stay apart during Hajj.

A city of tents is set up for pilgrims to stay in.

First, pilgrims enter the Great **Mosque** for **prayers**. They walk barefoot around the Ka'bah seven times, saying special prayers to Allah as they go.

Next, the pilgrims drink water from the Well of Zamzam. After that they walk or run seven times along the valley between the hills of Al-Safa and Al-Marwa. As they do this, they remember how Hajra ran there searching for water to save her baby son.

The valley between the hills used to be a dusty, open area crowded with shops and traffic. Now, it is a paved and covered corridor, so pilgrims are sheltered as they walk up and down it.

This plan shows the path pilgrims follow when on Hajj.

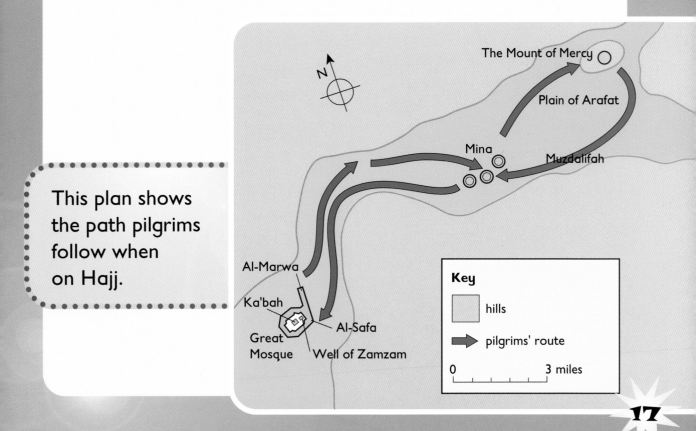

The Mount of Mercy

Plain of Arafat

Mina

Muzdalifah

Al-Marwa

Ka'bah

Al-Safa

Great Mosque

Well of Zamzam

Key

hills

pilgrims' route

0   3 miles

On Hajj beyond Mecca

Next, the **pilgrims** travel about 16 miles (25 kilometers) outside Mecca to Mount Arafat, the Mount of Mercy. There, they ask **Allah** to forgive their **sins.** This is called wuquf, or "standing before Allah." It is the most important part of **Hajj.** Pilgrims hope that Allah will forgive all the bad things they have done throughout their life.

The last stop of the Hajj is at Mina. This is where Satan, the devil, appeared to the **prophet** Ibrahim as he was trying to **pray.** Ibrahim threw seven pebbles at the devil, who then sank down defeated to the ground. The devil appeared twice more, and each time Ibrahim threw seven pebbles at him and defeated him. The three stone pillars at Mina are **symbols** of the devil. Pilgrims gather small pebbles to throw at the pillars to show that they reject the devil and his evil ways, as Ibrahim did long ago.

Pilgrims sit on Mount Arafat.

This is one of the stone pillars at Mina. Some of the pilgrims are throwing pebbles.

Id-ul-Adha is one of the main Muslim festivals. It falls during the Hajj. At this festival, Muslims remember how Ibrahim sacrificed a ram. You can read the story below. At Id-ul-Adha, pilgrims pay to give food to the poor.

At the end of the Hajj, pilgrims can relax a little after the simple life on Hajj.

Ibrahim and Isma'il

The **Qur'an** tells how Allah told Ibrahim to **sacrifice** his beloved son, Isma'il. Because he loved Allah, Ibrahim wanted to obey. Just in time, Ibraham heard the voice of Allah telling him to stop, and to sacrifice a ram instead of his son. Ibrahim had proved his love of Allah, and Isma'il was safe.

When I Went on Hajj

Hasina, a Muslim woman from Birmingham, England remembers going on **Hajj** to Mecca as a young woman.

*I saved all my money for the first year that I worked, until I could afford to go on Hajj. I traveled to Mecca with my brother and some other people from our **mosque.** I was worried, but excited too!*

At first, I was surprised that the Ka'bah was inside such a modern building. I expected to see more of the desert. But then, as I got used to it, tears came to my eyes and all my worries seemed to fall away.

African women pilgrims are arriving at Mecca.

This shows the outside of the Great Mosque in Mecca.

I felt very happy on Hajj. All the **prayers** and rituals help you to find peace inside yourself. God gives you strength to bear the great heat and crowds. The hardship makes you feel stronger. I worried less about ordinary things, such as what other people might be thinking. Everybody looks after one another.

We bought bottles of Zamzam water to take home as gifts. Being at home felt strange for a while, after such a simple life of prayer. Just talking about Hajj makes me long to be at Mecca again!

More about Islam

The Five Pillars of **Islam** are the five most important ways Muslims keep their religion. These are the five basic **beliefs** of Islam. All Muslims should follow each of the five beliefs.

Muslims usually go to the **mosque** to **pray,** although they can pray anywhere as long as it is clean. "All the world is a mosque," said the **prophet** Muhammad (**pbuh**).

At the mosque, men pray together in a large, open room. Women may pray in a different part of the room, in another room, or at home.

The Five Pillars of Islam

- **Faith:** Muslims believe that there is no God but **Allah,** and Muhammad (pbuh) is his prophet.
- Prayer: Muslims pray five times each day, facing Mecca.
- Charity: They give money to the poor.
- Fasting: They go without food or drink during daylight, throughout the month of Ramadan.
- **Pilgrimage:** They go on **Hajj** to Mecca. Muslims must do this once during their lifetime.

Muslim prayers follow a set pattern, with movements including bowing, kneeling, and bending down to touch the floor with your forehead. Different prayers are said in each position. Everyone moves and says the same prayers together. In their prayers, Muslims worship **Allah** and ask **blessings** for Muhammad (pbuh) and for all Muslims.

The most important Muslim prayer is called the shahada. Translated into English, it means:
There is no god but Allah and
Muhammad is the Messenger of Allah.

Children are learning in a class at a mosque.

Through the Muslim Year

The month of Ramadan is special to Muslims. Every year during Ramadan, Muslims fast. This means they do not eat or drink anything during the hours of sunlight. Muslims believe that it is good to have control over your body. Making yourself wait to eat, even when you are hungry, is one way of showing this control.

Fasting is a reminder that everyone is equal. Hunger is the same for everyone, whether they are rich or poor.

A family breaks their fast during Ramadan.

Muslim months and years

The Muslim calendar is based on the Moon, instead of the Sun and the seasons, like the Western calendar. The Muslim year is about eleven days shorter because each month is shorter. So each year, Muslim festivals fall on an earlier date according to the Western calendar.

At the end of the month of Ramadan is the festival of Id-ul-Fitr. This is a great celebration, when families gather together for a special meal to end the fast. People go to visit friends and relatives at Id-ul-Fitr. They may have new clothes to wear, and they bring small presents of candy or nuts for the children.

The Muslim New Year comes on the Day of the Hijrah. This is the first day of the Muslim month of Muharram. On this day, Muslims remember the journey made by Muhammad (**pbuh**) to Medinah.

The Moon rises over the **mosque** at Dubai, United Arab Emirates.

Other Muslim Holy Places: Medinah

Medinah is the second most important place for Muslims. It is known as the "city of light." Medinah is also in Saudi Arabia. It is about about 100 miles (320 kilometers) north of Mecca. Because it gets more rain than the harsh desert around Mecca, Medinah is green with many trees.

The story goes that when the **prophet** Muhammad (**pbuh**) arrived at Medinah, many people offered him shelter and land. But Muhammad (pbuh) did not want to be a burden to anyone and he did not want to seem to choose one person over everyone else. He said that he would build his own house on the spot where his camel decided to stop.

Medinah is cooler and greener than Mecca.

This mosque is built at the grave of Muhammad (pbuh).

Everyone followed the camel to see where it would stop. Then Muhammad (pbuh) bought that piece of land, and his followers helped him to build a house there.

When Muhammad (pbuh) died in 632 C.E., he was buried at Medinah. A beautiful **mosque** is built at the site of his grave. **Pilgrims** come to visit and **pray** there.

The first Hajj

Muhammad (pbuh) went to Medinah because the people of Mecca were angry. They did not want to follow his teaching. Then, six years later, he returned to Mecca and marched with his followers straight to the Ka'bah. At last, the people of Mecca accepted his teachings. This journey back to Mecca became the first pilgrimage, or **Hajj.**

Other Muslim Holy Places: Jerusalem

The Dome of the Rock is a mosque in Jerusalem.

Jerusalem, in the modern country of Israel, is the third most **holy** place for Muslims. A **mosque** with a golden dome, called the Dome of the Rock, is built where the **prophet** Muhammad (**pbuh**) was lifted up to heaven when he made his Night Journey.

Muhammad's Night Journey

It is said that one night in Mecca, the Angel Jibril visited the prophet Muhammad (pbuh). This time, Jibril brought a strange beast, called Buraq, for Muhammad (pbuh) to ride. Buraq had wings and could gallop faster than lightning. Muhammad (pbuh) mounted Buraq and in a single second he was taken to Jerusalem. He sat on Mount Moriah, where Ibrahim had bound Isma'il for **sacrifice.** Slowly, Muhammad (pbuh) rose to heaven. There, he talked to Aadam, Ibrahim, and Isa (Jesus). That is why Jerusalem is **sacred** for Muslims.

The Al-Aqsa mosque nearby has a silver dome. The two domes can be seen from all around Jerusalem. This is the spot where Muhammad (pbuh) is said to have landed after his Night Journey on Buraq.

Jerusalem is a holy city for **Jews** and **Christians** as well. Through the centuries, there have been times when people of different **religions** have lived and worshiped together peacefully there. But there has often been conflict, too. Today, people continue to fight in Jerusalem.

The Al-Aqsa Mosque stands in Jerusalem, facing the Dome of the Rock.

Glossary

Allah   Muslim name for God

beliefs   when you think or know something to be true

C.E.   stands for the Common Era. People of all religions can use this, instead of the Christian A.D. that counts from the birth of Jesus Christ. The year numbers are not changed.

Christian   someone who follows the religion of Christianity and the teachings of Jesus

faith   belief in God (Allah)

Hajj   Muslim name for the holy journey or pilgrimage to Mecca

Hebrew Bible   Jewish holy book

holy (holiest)   to do with God

Islam   religion of Muslims

Jews (Jewish)   someone who follows the religion of Judaism

Middle East   lands around the east and south of the Mediterranean Sea, including countries such as Saudi Arabia, Israel, Egypt, Iran, and Iraq

miracle   something that God made happen

mosque   Muslim place of worship, sometimes also called a masjid

muezzin   Muslim man who calls people to prayer

pbuh   letters stand for "peace be upon him"

pilgrimage journey made for religious reasons

pilgrim someone making a pilgrimage

pray/prayer to think about or talk to God (Allah). A prayer is the words you think or say when you pray.

prophet someone who tells people what God (Allah) wants

Qur'an Muslim holy book

religion (religious) belief in God or gods

sacrifice offering something to God (Allah)

sin doing something wrong, and going against the teachings of God (Allah)

symbol sign, or something that stands for something else

Index